D1616495

TINY HOUSE STYLE

ISBN Number: 978-0-692-26960-2
Written by Steve Weissmann and Jenna Spesard
Published: 2014
Tumbleweed Tiny House Company®

INTRODUCTION

Introduction

WHY ON A TRAILER? During the 1960s the government established a set of building codes that required households to meet a certain size and, in doing so, made tiny homes illegal. As time passed, more municipalities started enforcing citizens to live in larger and larger homes. But is bigger always better? The simple lifestyle desired by tiny home dwellers began to slip away...

But there was a loophole.

Flash forward. The year was 1999 when our first tiny home was mounted to a trailer. The little home was named Tumbleweed because it had roots and was mobile all at the same time. And in that moment, the seeds for a housing revolution were planted.

Today, international building code requires a home contain at least 220 square of interior space, and most municipalities actually call for higher limits. RVs and travel trailers are not restricted by these same laws. And so, a house on wheels isn't a house at all. Or it is?

Decide for yourself as you travel through these pages into 100–200 square feet. Let your creativity drive and encounter endless possibilities. Live beyond the limits and allow yourself to dream tiny.

By creating innovative charming houses on wheels,
we also cracked the building code.

Forward

When I first learned of Tumbleweed Tiny Houses, it wasn't something that I needed to research much. I've owned many vehicles, I live to ski and it was obvious that a Tiny House was the next step in the refinement of the ultimate ski bum's dream. In summers, I worked as a carpenter building large custom homes. I was a lover of natural materials with a skiers understanding of the possible life benefits of a portable living arrangement. I appreciate fine construction and wanted a tiny house for myself but most importantly, I had recently fallen in love. I had found a woman who shared my vision for a life spent neck deep in adventure.

The thing about women is almost all of them have mothers. There are few more difficult conversations a young women can have than explaining to her parents that she is moving in with her boyfriend who... lives in his van. When your girlfriend's parents find out that you don't pay rent, all the charisma in the world won't help you a bit. In my experience, only an extremely well built Tiny House can offer the same freedoms as a van yet side step the ever looming stigmas that follow the traveler.

As Tiny House dwellers, we wear our values on our sleeves. When people see my house, they know without asking that I am a person who values quality over quantity, a person who loves natural materials enough to not abuse them. I am a person who is willing to curb my own personal excess in the interest of expanding my personal freedom. They see a proud craftsman, an artist and an activist. I am unashamed of my choices and the confidence that comes with that knowledge, becomes my character.

I am a Tiny House dweller and, in turn, I have been surprised to find out that my favorite part of it all has been the connections I've made along the way. Rich and poor, conservative and liberal, young and old – the reasons for people's curiosity in my life are as assorted as my own motivations to live Tiny in the beginning. The people I've met and the community I am a part of have become the true currency of my personal wealth.

We are a tribe.

Tumbleweed Tiny Houses have made sense to me from the very first time I laid eyes on these adorable cabins on wheels. I didn't need to hear about the economic advantages, the environmental necessity of reevaluated building practices or the communal benefits.

Zack Giffin
Host, Tiny House Nation
Owner/Builder, Tumbleweed Home

"Happiness is not something you postpone for the future; it is something you design for the present." —Jim Rohn

Table of Contents

TOUR A HOUSE: Welcome to this Elm 24, now on display in downtown Las Vegas. It will get moved and lived-in soon.

TOUR A HOUSE

Tour A House

IMAGINE YOURSELF STANDING IN A ROOM NO LARGER THAN 172 SQUARE FEET. Pile in your cherished belongings and necessary home amenities. Decorate this space to express your personal style. Envision this room as your oasis, your dream house. And, notice as the walls begin to melt away.

In order for a tiny house to be mobile without a permit, the rules of the road require they be no taller than 13'6" and no wider than 8'6." Using those dimensions, our houses are artfully designed to allow space for you to live comfortably and without sacrifice.

Living tiny doesn't mean living without luxury. Fill your space with all the comforts of a traditional home:

Kitchen: Sauté, bake, and sear with a stovetop, full range, fridge, and freezer
Bathroom: Primp and cleanse with a hot shower, toilet, and sink
Sleeping Area: Cozy up with your partner, upstairs or down
Great Room: Kick up your feet or entertain in a variety of layouts
Plus: Air conditioners, heaters, and washer and dryer units are available

Our tiny homes are constructed the same as conventional homes—using 2x4 wall framing, double pane windows, and R-20 of insulation. They are as strong as they are alluring, but the real beauty of small-scaled construction is that it advocates for attention to detail.

Enter the Elm, breath easy, and enjoy a tickle of excitement. This sized down shelter looks and feels like a small traditional home.

The lancet window beautifully enkindles this Tumbleweed's front loft. An ideal space for festive decor, functional storage, or a comfy reading nook.

The great room melts into the kitchen. Catch a glimpse of the sleeping loft and back bedroom as you continue your tour.

A folding butcher block helps save space and can also double as a
dining table when entertaining.

Create a kitchen that reflects your personal cooking style. Do you prefer a stove top or full range? Gas or electric?

A traditional rolling library ladder saves space and adds a pinch of nostalgia. Go ahead, give it a climb.

You don't have to worry about bumping elbows with your partner—this loft is open and airy with dormers and five windows!

Journey back downstairs, and pass by a full closet and bathroom.
Arrive at the second sleeping nook straight ahead.

This cozy downstairs bedroom offers a private escape. One dreamer may nest in peace, either day or night.

As you travel back down the hall, check out Elm's adorable bathroom sink. Plenty of space underneath for toiletries. Pamper up!

This pragmatic bathroom includes all the essentials:
A flush toilet, shower, and sink.

EXTERIORS: This Cypress 20 is bathed in classic cedar siding, topped with a hipped green roof and matching window frames.

EXTERIORS

Exteriors

"We shape our buildings; thereafter they shape us."
—Winston Churchill

WHY DO WE LOVE TINY HOUSES? As with any home, your exterior establishes the first impression. In tiny house design, it also acts as a mold that will shape the entire sculpture.

Interior layout decisions, such as shower and sink placement, will be made based on your exterior composition. Windows sit in precise locations, so that sunlight can dance around your floor. Roofs peak, so that your ceiling can climb. Sculpt your shell to accommodate the future body within.

Key design elements from traditional architecture are also used when creating tiny homes. In the Elm, shown on the right, two windows are perfectly centered around the doorway. This balance creates an inviting entrance and forges a bright focal point with our custom door.

Speaking of our door, we've scaled it down to be proportional with the rest of the house. This tactic gives the Elm a feeling of wholeness and unifies not only the exterior but, also, the interior of the home.

As you continue your journey in the following pages, ask yourself: What type of tiny house exterior defines you?

Simple. Proportional. Balanced. This Elm 24 showcases traditional home design principals.

The Cypress features a side porch and a bright interior nook, surrounded by five luminescent windows.

From the front, the Cypress's adorable hipped roof creates balance. It's a familiar archetype in cottage homes.

The Linden sits pretty by an open field over looking majestic under the beautiful Colorado mountains and skyscrape.

As a bungalow, Linden's main roof runs 90 degrees across the home, sloping towards the front and back.

This Elm shows off classic perspective lines, full porch, and expanded loft dormers.

Our first Tumbleweed home (89 square feet) revolutionized tiny houses and inspired our larger present day Elm models.

Mica's modern design maximizes living space to 172 square feet, with a sliding glass door that allows your walls to drink in the sunshine.

Offering one level living and hot rolled steel siding,
the Mica is a smooth operator.

"Little Yellow" has a country-home appeal with it's enormous front window (Cypress 18).

"Bayside Bungalow" flaunts the design principal of hierarchy in her window placement—smaller above, larger below (Cypress 18).

While this Washington home travels in winter, its board and batten
siding "weathers the storm" just fine.

In Louisiana, one tiny house features 100-year-old cypress siding and a wide open porch layout.

EXTERIOR DETAILS: From the color of the roof to the thickness of window trim, the devil is always in the details!

EXTERIOR DETAILS

Exterior Details

"Making the simple complicated is commonplace; making the complicated simple, awesomely simple, that's creative."
—Charles Mingus

WHAT SETS TINY HOUSES APART? Details create the melody of your home's musical composition. First, envision a beautiful song. Listen as it plays out in your head. Only then, can you begin to pick your notes.

The siding you choose will punctuate your style and act as an elegant armor, welcoming your guests while protecting your abode. We've chosen cedar siding for many of our homes because it is: warm and rich, strong and light weight, resistant to insects, and, most of all, universally adored.

By contrast, our Mica's hot rolled steel siding has a modern appeal. The industrial metal creates a natural patina that guards against the outside elements, while turning your home into a contemporary beauty.

If a tiny home's exterior were to perform a ballet, color would take center stage. When bathed in natural tones, a tiny home will inspirit the environmentalist. Rose-colored window shutters will bring forth a blushing beauty, while a yellow door will glow and entice.

One of the most amazing benefits of tiny house design is that people are able to make it their own. By combining design preferences and personal touches, a cacophony becomes a symphony, and a tiny house becomes a extension of its owner.

A simple classic porch light makes a elegant statement as
it beckons you home.

A spa-like door illuminates the interior, and was specifically sought out and trimmed to fit this tiny home.

Revisiting the porch from our first Tumbleweed (1999), you feel a little bit of the "Wild West" in the deep weathered wood.

Porch decorations and furniture can pepper an overall tone
or make a statement.

Why have a typical porch post? Find a large branch and incorporate nature in your exterior design.

Window trim can whisper or shout! Subtle trim (shown here)
displays a refined simplicity.

Charismatic window trim (shown here, ablaze in color)
pops with vivacity.

Hot rolled steel with a weathered patina creates
an industrial look for the Mica.

In this Elm, silver trim flashes a smile above a lancet window,
creating an inviting aesthetic.

Symmetry is discretely delivered with a burgundy accent color mimicked on the door and window grids.

Sliding glass doors create deliver an ocean-view triptych in the Mica,
accentuated with a bold red trim.

GREAT ROOM: A multi-functional room designed to facilitate your unique lifestyle.

GREAT ROOMS

Great Rooms

"One can furnish a room very luxuriously by taking out furniture rather than putting it in."
—Francis Jourdain

CAN A GREAT ROOM FIT IN A TINY HOUSE? Absolutely.

To you—it's the hub for relaxation, work, and play. To your tiny house—it's the epicenter, the core, the soul.

Step into your great room. A morning song rides the breeze as it enters through numerous windows. Vaulted ceilings reach for blue skies as the sun ignites a heavenly skylight. Relax in your sitting area or while settling into a work desk, comfortable in a space made specifically for you.

The great room is the most important room in any house, and no two are the same. Designed to accompany your lifestyle, great rooms can be an open book or divided into chapters. Host a small dinner party in an open layout that envelopes the kitchen, or create virtual room dividers by keeping it separate while adding an office or den.

Give your great room life and it will blossom. Flip through the following pages, and envision how particular designs could enhance your daily routine. You deserve a space that caters to your way of life, not the other way around.

In this 24-ft long Elm, the great room envelopes the kitchen, creating an open layout.

This great room/kitchen combo arrangement visually lengthens
an 18-ft Cypress

The front alcove of this Cypress is a dreamy spot to curl up with a good book.

This open layout allows the cook to join in on the sitting room fun!
Notice the fold out counter extension, perfect for dining or food prep.

Small comfortable furniture does exist! Hunt for the right sizes and
shapes, or if your handy, build your own.

A wrought iron bistro table and chairs makes a wonderful dining set for two.

A screen divider can create a separate room or
fold away when extra space is needed.

In this Elm, the great room consolidates with the kitchen and allows for two entryway closets and an additional room in the back.

Additional den/office made possible by Elm's consolidated kitchen/great room.

KITCHENS: When preparing dinner you can absorb a gorgeous sunset through these brilliant bay windows.

KITCHENS

Kitchens

"You know you have reached perfection of design not when you have nothing more to add, but when you have nothing more to take away."
—Antoine de Saint-Exupéry

WILL A KITCHEN MEET ALL MY NEEDS? Absolutely.

A Tiny Recipe:
Mix a unique sink, stove top, and mini refrigerator in a large bowl. Flavor with colorful cabinets. Add a dash of storage to taste. Blend until you have a consistency that is confident and functional. Let stand on your one-of-a-kind countertop.

A tiny kitchen can accommodate any chef. Pick and choose your required ingredients: propane or electric stove top, range oven, full size or mini refrigerator, and even a washer/dryer combination unit! Add a pinch of personal style with baskets, mason jars, a magnetized spice rack for your fridge, burlap bags, and custom cabinets with intricate knobs.

Whether you're a culinary expert or simply a food admirer, creating a stylish serviceable kitchen is the recipe for a successful meal. Gather and measure ingredients, season to taste, and voila—you'll create a beautiful cook space as your signature dish. Bon Appetite!

Colors and patterns sizzle in this Cypress owner's eclectic kitchen sink.

Clean up is a piece of cake with electric-powered cook tops, while propane will simmer off-grid with ease.

This "Dream" kitchen proudly showcases a stunningly spacious
L-shaped countertop.

Placing the cooktop and sink nearby makes preparing tasty dishes a little easier.

Stainless steel glistens in this tiny kitchen, while a full gas range ignites your inner chef.

Black and white kitchen features emit a sophisticated aura in our modern Mica.

By contrast, this Cypress owner's live edge wood countertop and circular sink has a country home feel.

Imagine basking in the summer breeze while you slice and dice! High shelves add extra storage while reducing clutter.

This warm kitchen features space saving hook storage for pots and pans.

SLEEPING SPACES: This spacious upstairs bedroom offers privacy, comfort and star gazing views for two.

SLEEPING SPACES

Sleeping Spaces

"You know you're in love when you can't fall asleep because reality is finally better than your dreams."
—Dr. Seuss

IS THERE ENOUGH ROOM TO SLEEP? You spend about one third of your life asleep, so the space you choose to snooze should comfortably assist you into a deep relaxing slumber.

In a tiny home most sleeping spaces are intimately lofted to allow for space below. Canoodle in a queen size bed, drift away under skyward sloping ceilings, and listen as a fresh spring rain pitter-patters on the roof overhead.

The world is big and beautiful, often we forget until we look out the window. Thrust your bedroom out into nature by installing a skylight. Learn all the constellations as you snuggle under the cosmos. Wake early to admire an angelic sunrise, or sleep in to savor a dream.

Optional dormers will give your bedroom a spacious wingspan, allowing you to soar towards shuteye in a luxurious king size bed. With the extra space, you can add colorful nightstands, bookcases, storage, or even a small hobby area.

Downstairs dreaming is also made possible in tiny homes with murphy beds and convertible couches. Not only do they save on space, but they allow non-climbers to hibernate with ease.

Two can sleep under the stars in this cozy loft space, highlighted with a gorgeous skylight.

Travel down the hall to the Mica's spacious first floor bedroom.

Overhead cabinets and under bed storage add a practical value to the Mica's bright contemporary style.

A large murphy bed is used in this Cypress Arise's downstairs bedroom.
When folded away, it also doubles as an additional space.

A sunny additional downstairs bedroom allows for three dreamers to sleep in this Elm with ease.

The loft with shed style dormers, opens up the sleeping space and lets the light shine in.

Drift off under a crescent moon with the addition of a skylight (or two)!

STORAGE: Tiny home owners can tote a surprising amount storage by being resourceful and inventive with their space.

STORAGE

Storage

"Have nothing in your house that you do not know to be useful or believe to be beautiful."
—William Morris

HOW MUCH STORAGE IS JUST ENOUGH? Planning your tiny home's storage is a creative journey. Think of it as a lively puzzle that, when solved, will grant boundless improvements on your daily life.

A tiny house will allow for storage in more innovative ways than you ever thought possible, but a small space is most enjoyable when free of clutter. Cleanse yourself of items you hardly use. Now, begin to weave a cohesive flow between your shelter, your belongings, and your routine.

There's no wrong way to store, so challenge yourself to think outside the box. Invent ways to contain your goods while adding character to your home. Use ornate hooks instead of bulky hangers. Create corner shelves and cabinets. Place items inside baskets that double as decor. Elevate your bed to add hidden drawers underneath.

Free yourself from clutter. Engineer your space to cleverly accent your belongings. Let the burden of disorganization slide off your shoulders, and proudly float through your home with lightness.

Built-ins create storage in the Mica bedroom, with full set of shelves and an enclosed bottom cabinet.

Open shelves in this great room are perfect for displaying your favorite books and family photos.

Storage encircles this tiny kitchen. Don't be afraid to install shallow shelves, used here as a spice store.

Store snow covered coats and boots in this closet placed near the entryway.

Build a display for your favorite belongings, and storage can double as lovely decor.

This additional bedroom provides an elevated single bed and...

An enormous hidden storage for larger possessions!

In the loft, triangular corner shelves can double as nightstands to hold your books, glasses, blankets, etc.

Kitchens, in their very essence require "stuff"—pots, pans, plates, etc. Plenty of shelving can help reduce clutter on your counters.

INTERIOR DETAILS: Colors and patterns can guide the eye to a vibrant focal point or help a camouflage by blending with the walls.

INTERIOR DETAILS

Interior Details

"You can design and create, and build the most wonderful place in the world. But it takes people to make the dream a reality."
—Walt Disney

WHAT SETS A TINY HOUSE APART? The simple answer is you! You are one-of-a-kind, and like an all-encompassing accessory, a tiny house will embody your unique spirit.

As you decorate, add hints of your individuality to the walls. Knobs and hinges breathe life into a door or drawer. Rusted copper hardware will whisper industrial charm, while sleek steel will sing modernity. Let these details give your house a voice.

Notes of your particular heritage or interests can write a story. Feature a few keepsakes as part of your decor, and listen as your house completes the novel for you. For instance, if you love travel or have an affinity for sailing, find a nautical light fixture or frame an old map.

Use color as a feast for the eyes or wet the appetite with vibrant accents. Bring nature inside with floral patterns and organic materials. Elongate a room by using horizontal stripes, or make it feel tall by accentuating the ceiling.

A tiny house will grow and change with you. Delicate drapes will giggle along with your charismatic laugh. Polished knobs will dance while you sway to your favorite song. And plush pillows will softly cuddle while you dissolve into a dream.

A simple knotted rope ties back these lime curtains, adding a finishing touch with a homey quality.

These polished wood steps rotate around a pole to become a ladder alternative and staple of this tiny abode.

Rolling, library ladders are now standard for loft access in Tumbleweed houses, providing stability and flexibility.

Details make a statement. Hang your towels on decorative ornate hooks to add a touch of personality.

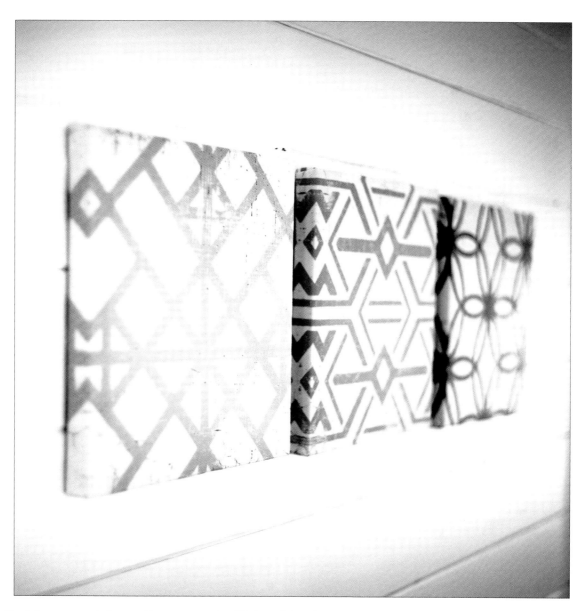

Bold geometric patterns embellish white horizontal panels in this great room.

The Mica is outfitted in slick modern ethos, right down to its door knob hardware and solid black counter tops.

A woven bamboo kitchen shade is simple, stylish, and adds a hint of exotic. A deep stainless steel sink makes doing dishes a breeze.

This poised metal and glass chandelier—standard in Tumbleweeds—
bounces light off the ceiling to create a soft pleasing illumination.

Another standard fixture in our lofts and kitchens creates artistic patterns while producing a bright warm glow.

This sculptural, copper switch plate is a piece of everyday art.

A nautical mirror adds a touch of adventure to this tiny bathroom, while an unfurling branch doubles as a jewelry hanger.

Sprinkle the wall with your favorite decorations; swap them out when you find something new. Your decor will evolve with you, and that's half the fun!

This rustic metal door hinge adds strength to the classic vintage style of this tiny home.

UNMENTIONABLES: Control your home's temperature with air conditioning, powered by this external compressor.

UNMENTIONABLES

Unmentionables

"Design is not just what it looks like and feels like. Design is how it works."
—Steve Jobs

WHEN CAN WE DISCUSS PLUMBING? If you look under the skirt of any tiny home, you'll meet a few unsung heroes. Masters of light, water, and temperature control; these fellas fly the aircraft, so you can enjoy the inflight movie. But the best part? When it comes to your utility bill, your house isn't the only thing that's tiny!

Tiny homes on wheels are constructed to mimic the luxury and ease of a structural home, but with the mobility of an RV. With a simple extension cord, propane tank, and water hose, you can fire up in your own backyard or plug-in at a campground. A few modifications such as: a solar panel system, composting toilet, and holding tanks for showers and sinks, can enable an off-grid lifestyle.

When you need to "do your business," tiny homes offer either a flush toilet or a composting unit (for off-grid). A water-based flusher will require a black water tank for sewage and an occasional pump out—the same as an RV or connect to the sewer, while composting units use peat moss or sawdust to breakdown your waste.

When outfitted with the correct "unmentionables", these silent worker bees will add comfort and serenity to your daily routine, while slashing your utility bills.

Your electrical framework will include an exterior outlet. Plug into a permanent power source or a 50 amp generator.

On the trailer hitch, the air conditioning compressor unit is located to the left and a propane tank to the right.

It's time to see your water heater vent (right),
water hose hookup (center) and external power jack.

Under this sink, you will find a water tank which holds 26 gallons and other pipes for drainage.

Like any home, this panel contains your circuit breakers. A small box will fulfill all your energy needs.

In a Tumbleweed, you may install and use a flush toilet which is plugged into a sewer, septic, or RV park hook-up.

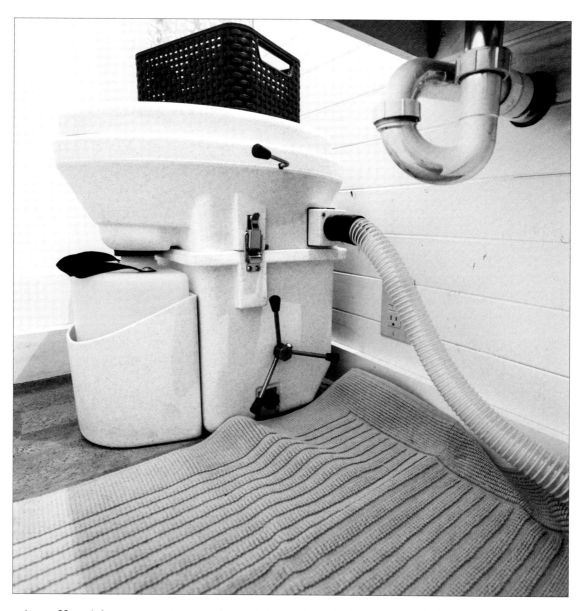

An off-grid compost unit, like this Nature's Head model, separates your deposits using peat moss. It's not stinky!

Store your toiletries in a cute basket to beautify your space—in this unit a simple composting toilet.

Your bathroom might be small, but that doesn't mean you can't transform it into a teeny spa!

ENVIRONMENTS: A tiny home trotting down the highway, engulfed by a snowy alpine landscape.

ENVIRONMENTS

Environments

"If you have built castles in the air, your work need not be lost; that is where they should be. Now put the foundations under them."
—Henry David Thoreau

DO TINY HOUSES TRAVEL OR ESTABLISH ROOTS? Both.

Snowflakes fall on a Tumbleweeds that have found roots in Alaska. Waves crash near homes that soak permanently in the warm California sun. Wheels turn as tiny abodes travel seasonally from the Great Lakes to the Gulf.

Small shelters are used in a variety of ways, including part-time vacation and pleasure. Tiny homes greet travelers as inviting guest homes and cozy rentable cottages. Entrepreneurs employ them as a separate office or studio. Families fill their walls with laughter on unforgettable road trips.

Whether your tiny home sprouts roots in pastoral Montana or nestles proudly in bustling New York City, you'll have the freedom to move, change, and grow. Tiny homes exist solely to enhance your lifestyle and to assist in fulfilling your dreams. There's no wrong way to use this space.

Flexibility. Freedom. Possibility. Seek out your life, and let your home guide you.

In Northern California, "Little Yellow" sits in a field with rolling hills and the pacific ocean nearby.

Another winter day dawns in the tiny ski house, which offers warmth in extreme climates.

Hard-core skiers yearn to sleep near the lifts. A hunger now made full by a tiny mobile house.

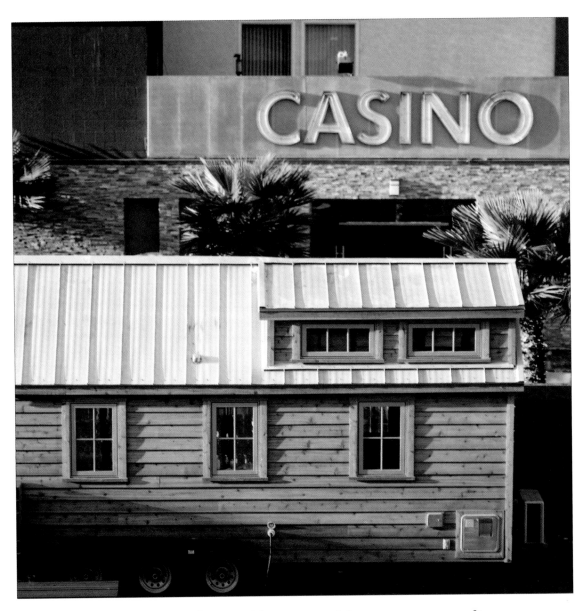

Our Elm 24 savors the Las Vegas sunshine on a sunny afternoon.

Later, this same little house dances in Downtown Vegas's neon lights.

One customized Tumbleweed Elm sits in Washington state, sporting an extra-special porch.

This customized Cypress, located on the Puget Sound,
functions as a vacation rental.

The Elm house at dusk, is showered with twinkling lights
to celebrate the holidays.

Several Tumbleweeds reside around a plastic ice rink in Las Vegas.
One serves as the skate rental shop.

FINALE: Tumbleweed Tiny House Company welcomes you to the enormous world of tiny homes. Come back soon, we'll leave a light on.

FINALE